GROUP READING GUIDE

PROMISE AND HOPE

KATHY HENDRICKS

TWENTY-THIRD PUBLICATIONS
twentythirdpublications.com

Twenty-Third Publications
One Montauk Avenue, Suite 200, New London, CT 06320
(860) 437-3012 • (800) 321-0411 • www.twentythirdpublications.com

ISBN: 978-1-62785-549-5
Printed in the U.S.A.

bayard A division of Bayard, Inc.

HOW TO USE THIS STUDY GUIDE

— SMALL GROUP SESSIONS —

Gather. Welcome everyone to your group. Ask participants to introduce themselves if needed.

As your class or group session gets underway, begin with the Sign of the Cross. Offer an appropriate psalm or other prayer together. Ask God to bless your time together and send the Spirit to guide you.

Read. Moving around the circle in your group, read aloud the material for the particular session. Rotate readers with each paragraph. Pause for quiet reflection before entering into discussion and prayer.

Discuss and Pray. When you come to the group process notes, continue around the circle, discussing or praying as the notes direct. Use the guide's suggestions as a starting point and add your own questions, prayers, or action plans.

Finish. As you come to the end of your process, invite participants to identify the one or two large ideas that they will take away from your time together. Each participant may hear the material differently; there are no "correct" answers.

Conclude your session with a brief prayer and hospitality. Remind participants of the time and date of the next gathering.

SESSIONS

SESSION ONE

INTRODUCTION — Promise and Hope in Pastoral Theology

In preparation for this session, all participants are asked to read pages 1–29 before the session.

By way of introduction, Bill Huebsch describes a developing awareness of pastoral theology since Vatican II that has continued with successive papacies. It is an awareness concerned with the human person and shaped by the person of Jesus Christ. Its outcomes are "to heal people and restore their hope, to invite and welcome people into the Church in Jesus' name, and to help people become adult Christians of mature faith" (page 3).

FOR REFLECTION AND DISCUSSION: *What is your reaction to this theology? Does your heart say "yes," or "yes… but?" What has been your experience as a minister as well as one being ministered to?*

PART 1 – Points of Orientation for Pastoral Theology *(page 7)*

***Regarding the segment "Encounter with the Person of Jesus"** (pages 8–10)*

Bill Huebsch describes the first point of orientation as one leading to an encounter with Jesus Christ. In turn, such an encounter animates all of our ministerial efforts. "All pastoral ministry flows from the life and ministry of Jesus Christ. Therefore, when we enact pastoral ministry we do so under the power of grace with Jesus acting through us" (page 10).

FOR DISCUSSION: *In what way have you been touched by the love and mercy of Christ? How do you reflect that love and mercy through your pastoral leadership?*

***Regarding the segment "Sinners Leading Other Sinners to Mercy"** (pages 10–14)*

The second point of orientation is an awareness of our own sinfulness and belief in the limitless mercy of God. Drawing upon the account of the woman caught in the act of adultery (John 8:8–11), Huebsch emphasizes the need to see the person rather than the sin. He writes, "What strikes me in this story is the amount of silence the storyteller includes....In that silence the forgiveness and mercy of God became the resounding message" (page 14).

FOR DISCUSSION: *How have you known the need in your life for the healing touch of Jesus? What does this gospel passage—particularly the way in which Jesus remains silent for a time—say to you about parish ministry? Why is it so important to be a listening presence to others as part of your ministry?*

Regarding the segment "Personalist Theology" (pages 15–16)

The third point of orientation is a reminder of the person-to-person approach of pastoral ministry. This requires a way of relating to parishioners on an individual basis and respecting each person's journey of faith.

FOR DISCUSSION: *Given the various demands of work in a parish, how realistic is this approach? What would it take to make your ministerial efforts more personal?*

Regarding the segment "Liturgy is the Source and Summit" (pages 17–18)

The fourth point of orientation is on the centrality of the Eucharist in the life of the community. While our faith entails a personal encounter with Jesus Christ, it is also essentially communal. "Everything leads us time and again back to the table of the Lord" (page 17).

FOR DISCUSSION: *What place does the Eucharist hold in your parish? In what way does each ministry flow into and out of the liturgy, leading us back to the Lord's table?*

Regarding the segment "The Paschal Mystery" (pages 19–20)

The fifth point of orientation centers on the Paschal Mystery. As Huebsch notes, a profound encounter with Christ often comes through the suffering that is part of bereavement, loss, failure, and ruptured relationships.

FOR DISCUSSION: *How have you experienced hope springing from despair, life from death, light from a dark and desperate time? In what way has your own experience of the Paschal Mystery influenced the way you attend to those who are suffering in your parish?*

Regarding the segment "God is Still Speaking" (pages 20–21)

The sixth point of orientation is the ongoing revelation of God in our day-to-day lives. Learning to listen, through prayerful discernment, is a continual process. It is one that leads us not only to look for the direction God is giving to us, but also to consider the way in which we might help others seek and find guidance in their own lives.

FOR DISCUSSION: *How would you assess the spiritual offerings in your parish, especially those that focus on prayer and discernment?*

Regarding the segment "Grace" *(pages 21–22)*

The seventh point of orientation is the free-flowing nature of God's grace, which animates all efforts toward ministering to and with others. Pope Francis described grace as something beyond our consciousness and "the amount of light in our souls, not knowledge nor reason."

FOR DISCUSSION: *Name a time when you have found just the right words or response to a pastoral situation. In what ways would you attribute that response to this unconscious reality of grace?*

Regarding the segment "An Illustration" *(pages 24–29)*

An encounter works two ways. The story of John and Mary Ellen illustrates how the process of accompaniment flips when we open ourselves to the other.

FOR DISCUSSION: *Think of a time in which your ministry resulted in an encounter that flipped your assumptions and led to something unexpected. How did it affect your approach to pastoral ministry?*

FINAL REFLECTION AND DISCUSSION: *Revisit the first question about your initial reaction to pastoral theology. Has it changed as a result of going through the material in this chapter? How do the seven points of orientation give you a better appreciation for this theology?*

SESSION 2

PART 2 – Guidelines for Accompaniment *(page 31)*

In preparation for this session, all participants are asked to read pages 31–85 before the session.

This chapter offers twelve guidelines for accompanying others in their lives and experiences of faith. It begins with a reference to Pope Francis' image of the Church as a "field hospital." This requires, as Huebsch notes, a radical rethinking of parish life and opening our doors "to all who are wounded or suffering in their lives, regardless of their 'legal standing' in the Church" (page 32).

FOR REFLECTION AND DISCUSSION: *What does it mean to rethink parish life in a radical way? How does this challenge you? What does it affirm for you?*

Regarding the segment "How We Select and Interpret Scripture" *(pages 33–37)*
Because pastoral theology is grounded in the person and example of Jesus, it is vital to read Scripture with an open and receptive mind and heart. To this end, Huebsch offers several tools for interpreting biblical texts wisely.

FOR DISCUSSION: *Why is it so important to read Scripture in exegetical fashion? How might you incorporate these tools for reading Scripture into your pastoral leadership and service to the parish?*

Regarding the segment on "Offering Radical Availability" *(pages 37–40)*

The first guideline for the art of accompaniment is making ourselves available to parishioners with "a warm welcome and a heart full of mercy" (page 39). Such an approach calls for moving from the kind of reactivity that can characterize too much "doing" in a parish to one of responsiveness to parishioners' needs.

FOR DISCUSSION: *How realistic is it to make yourself available to the people in your parish? What changes would need to be made to your ministry in order to follow this guideline?*

Regarding the segment "Mercy First" *(pages 40–43)*

Drawing upon the account of Zacchaeus, Huebsch underscores the compassionate way in which Jesus regarded every human being. This, in turn, challenges us to see others as God sees them: as precious members of the body of Christ, worthy of love, devotion, and acceptance.

FOR DISCUSSION: *Recall and share about a time when someone treated you with the merciful love of Christ. How is your parish a model of mercy? In what ways could it grow to be more accepting of all its members?*

Regarding the segments "Mitigating Circumstances" *(pages 43–44)* ***and "People Come First"*** *(pages 45–47)*

Setting norms, expectations, and guidelines for various ministries and programs is an essential way to keep programs such as sacramental preparation on track. Adhering too strictly to these, however—for example, by seeing every person or household as identical in their capacity to participate—makes a parish rigid. Paying attention to mitigating circumstances requires a limber approach to ministry that is caring, receptive, and gracious.

FOR DISCUSSION: *How do you strike a balance between expectations around the involvement of your parishioners and the mitigating circumstances that inhibit that involvement? How does putting people first change the way we minister to others?*

Regarding the segment "Gradualism" (*pages 47–50*)

If you have ever felt frustrated over the slow response to a ministerial initiative, take heart from the experience of Jesus. His disciples were pretty slow on the uptake when it came to many of his teachings. As Huebsch notes, "If Jesus' own chosen team was having trouble understanding and following him, why do we expect our sisters and brothers today to follow immediately and perfectly?" (page 48). A recognition of the gradual way in which we grow in faith is essential for a pastoral approach to ministry.

FOR DISCUSSION: *How does this guideline for accompaniment strike you? Does it bring a sense of relief or heighten a sense of frustration? How might you grow more patient with those to whom you minister so that you can take them for where they are rather than where you expect them to be?*

Regarding the segment "A Hermeneutical Activity" (*pages 50–55*)

Through another illustration, Huebsch explains a hermeneutic approach to discernment—i.e., helping a seeker "read and interpret their experience through accompaniment, mercy, and healing" (page 50). The story of Clare and Dave distinguishes between different forms of inquiry. Forming salient questions guides a seeker toward attentiveness to God's voice in the formation of their own conscience.

FOR DISCUSSION: *What does it mean to be "trained in the art of accompaniment"? In what ways are you able or unable to utilize the various forms of inquiry within your pastoral leadership?*

Regarding the segment "To Integrate and Restore People to Full Life in the Church" (*pages 55–60*)

Huebsch acknowledges the tension that can exist between a pastoral response and a legal one. As with the guidelines on mitigating circumstances and putting people first, this one entails a more generous approach to ministry. "In short, we must 'make room for God's unconditional love in our pastoral activity'" (page 58).

FOR DISCUSSION: *In what ways are you "making room" for ministry in your parish? Where might you expand your efforts?*

Regarding the segment "Authentic Accompaniment" (pages 60–66)

The account of Zacchaeus once again provides insights into the way in which we accompany others as Jesus did. Such an approach involves accepting others without judgment, listening to their stories, and helping them discern God's voice and guidance in their lives.

FOR DISCUSSION: *Read the account of Zacchaeus (Luke 19:1–10). How might you apply Jesus' way of accompaniment to your ministry?*

Regarding the segment "The Power of Darkness" (pages 66–70)

In Mark's gospel, Jesus explains that there is nothing outside of us that defiles us, "but the things that come from within are what defile" (Mark 7:15). Huebsch underscores this by describing the need to "be in a constant state of discernment about our own work" (page 68). An honest recognition of our own failings, biases, and weaknesses brings us into a humble recognition of who we are and why we are called to ministry.

FOR DISCUSSION: *Call to mind any resentment, irritation, or anger you have held against someone else. How has this prevented you from being a compassionate presence in that person's life?*

Regarding the segment "The Servant to the Community" (pages 70–75)

One of the first images we had of Pope Francis after his election was that of him riding in a bus as he returned to his hotel to pay his bill. From the very start, he proved to be a model of servant leadership. Such is the model we are all called to follow in our approach to ministry.

FOR DISCUSSION: *When have you experienced servant leadership—either as one on the receiving or on the giving end? How has that influenced your approach to pastoral leadership?*

***Regarding the segments "Conscience"** (pages 75–83)*
***and "The Call to Holiness"** (pages 84–85)*

"Our consciences are our deepest sanctuaries, where we find our truest selves. They are that place where God reveals our destiny and purpose" (pages 76–77). Helping others to form, discern, and act out of their conscience is an essential aspect of accompaniment. As a sort of inner compass, our conscience not only guides us toward good choices but also draws us into holiness in "living the way God created us to live" (page 84).

FOR DISCUSSION: *How does Huebsch's definition of conscience expand, challenge, or affirm your own understanding? What has influenced the development of your conscience? How are you living a holy life?*

FINAL REFLECTION AND DISCUSSION: *Which of the guidelines for accompaniment speak most strongly to you? Which ones challenge you? How might you focus on one or two as you increase your capacity for accompaniment?*

SESSION 3

PART 3 – The People of God Seeking to Be Accompanied *(page 87)*

In preparation for this session, all participants are asked to read pages 87–96 before the session.

This chapter focuses on those seeking accompaniment as well as on both formal and informal means for walking with others along the spiritual path. Because it is the shortest chapter in the book, you might want to combine your discussion with session 4.

FOR REFLECTION AND DISCUSSION: *Reflect in quiet on a time when someone accompanied you. How would you characterize the kind of accompaniment you needed at that time?*

Regarding the segments "Within the Parish" and "Outside the Parish" *(pages 88–90)*
In this opening section Huebsch underscores the importance of intentional practice when it comes to accompanying others. All too often, parish programs and ministries depend on those coming to us. In doing so, we might assume that we are serving them well without being mindful of the ways in which we might provide welcome and accompaniment. It can then be easy to overlook the reasons for disin-

terest or disengagement. "About certain matters, many people have stopped coming to the Church for help because we have failed to accompany them well" (page 88).

FOR DISCUSSION: *How might you provide guidance in helping volunteers in various ministries to accompany others in their walk of faith? Consider the reasons why some parishioners remain disengaged. Do you agree or disagree with Huebsch's statement that they may not have been accompanied well?*

Regarding the segment "Category 1" on primary household relationships (pages 90–92)

In this section Huebsch distinguishes between the "regulars" and the "irregulars," with the latter living in situations that vary from the teaching of the Church. Both groups, however, pose a challenge when it comes to the spectrum of family needs. The excerpt from *The Joy of Love* emphasizes the need for mercy, understanding, and empathy when rising to meet these challenges.

FOR DISCUSSION: *On a scale of 1 (low) to 5 (high) how welcoming is your parish to both the regular and irregular households? When it comes to accompanying the people in your parish, what are you most proud of? Where might you improve your efforts?*

Regarding the segment "Category 2: Discernment of what God is asking in other areas of the faith" (pages 92–96)

Category 2 includes five groups that typify different ways to engage with the parish: the seekers, the silent, the absent, the morally self-assured, and the religiously self-assured. Each group requires a varying approach to accompaniment as well as evangelization.

FOR DISCUSSION: *Of the five groups named in category two, which challenge you the most in your ministry? Which ones have been responsive to your pastoral leadership? To what do you attribute the latter?*

FINAL REFLECTION AND DISCUSSION: *Who in your parish are those being best served through ministries and programs? Which groups need more attention? Identify one way you might strengthen your efforts to accompany one of the groups in category two.*

SESSION 4

PART 4 – Theological Reflection as the Method for Accompaniment *(page 97)*

In preparation for this session, all participants are asked to read pages 97–109 before the session.

This chapter describes the process of theological reflection and offers several models for putting it into practice. Taking these models, Huebsch then develops a schema for applying theological reflection to the role of accompanist.

FOR REFLECTION AND DISCUSSION: *Name an experience in which you were accompanied in your walk of faith. Who accompanied you? How did they do it? Was it a formal experience, such as spiritual direction, or an informal one? How comfortable do you feel in accompanying others in their walk of faith?*

Regarding the segment "The Need for Theological Reflection" *(pages 98–101)*
We live in reactive times. Internet access to news-in-the-making keeps us on edge and creates a distorted sense of reality. The call to interpret the signs of the times in light of the gospel is as vital now as it was when first issued in the Vatican II document *Pastoral Constitution on the Church in the Modern World*. Theological reflection provides an avenue toward a loving, merciful, and just response, both

to the pressing issues of our time as well as to our personal discernment. Huebsch describes how this process enables us to "step back from the din of life to contemplate quietly all that is in our hearts and souls" (page 100).

FOR DISCUSSION: *What is your experience with theological reflection? How might it be helpful as a process for discerning a response to the "signs of the times"?*

Regarding the segment on "Models of Theological Reflection" (pages 101–105)

This section describes differing models for theological reflection. While varied in approach, there is a thread of continuity running through their common use of Scripture, personal experience, and invitations to deeper reflection.

FOR DISCUSSION: *With which of the models do you have experience? Which one appeals the most to you? How do you see yourself using one or more of the models in your approach to accompaniment and as part of your pastoral leadership?*

Regarding the segment "Our Blend: Theological reflection in pastoral accompaniment" (pages 105–109)

Drawing upon the various models, Huebsch pulls together a method of accompaniment for use within a pastoral setting. He then describes how these "swim together" in actual practice, making the process applicable in a particular way to pastoral ministry.

FOR DISCUSSION: *What appeals to you about this approach to accompaniment? In what ways might you draw upon the blended method as part of your parish approach to accompaniment? Is there any part that you find overwhelming or unrealistic? How might you tailor it to make the approach usable in your parish situation?*

FINAL REFLECTION AND DISCUSSION: *How might you integrate one of the models of theological reflection into your own spirituality? Do you find yourself drawn to one or more as a way to deepen your spiritual life and relationship with Christ?*

SESSION 5

PART 5 – The Person Who Is the Accompanist and the Process of Accompaniment *(page 111)*

In preparation for this session, all participants are asked to read pages 111–148 before the session.

This chapter focuses on the person who serves as the accompanist and names eight steps for carrying out the process of accompaniment. Each one is grounded in an approach based on theological reflection and pastoral ministry as a personalized endeavor.

FOR REFLECTION AND DISCUSSION: *How does your faith impact the manner in which you serve as a pastoral leader? How have you been challenged by your faith to change, alter, or strengthen the way you minister to and with others?*

Regarding the segment "Step 1: Be Close to Jesus" (pages 112–114)

Huebsch notes that serving as an accompanist is a calling that often coincides with the call to pastoral leadership. This makes the need for authenticity essential for those involved in parish ministry. He also notes that not everyone who is baptized, ordained, or in consecrated life is prepared to serve as an accompanist.

FOR DISCUSSION: *After reading through the attributes of an authentic accompanist, which ones most strongly describe you? Which ones do you need to strengthen or expand upon? How do you feel called to accompany others?*

Regarding the segment on "Step 2: Radical Availability" (pages 114–115)

Unlike the programmatic aspects of parish work, accompaniment doesn't run on a particular timetable. It calls for accessibility and availability. It also requires sensitivity toward those who genuinely seek accompaniment as well as the recognition that one's efforts may not always result in a response.

FOR DISCUSSION: *Given the other demands of your ministerial role, how realistic is it to be "radically available"? How might you readjust some of your responsibilities so as to be more accessible to those you serve?*

Regarding the segments "Step 3: Telling the Story and Step 4: Listening to the Story" (pages 115–118)

It's a sad reality of our times that many people know more about the story of a famous celebrity than they do of their own inner lives. The art of accompaniment encourages seekers to reflect upon their experiences and, in doing so, tell their own story. Active listening on the part of the accompanist entails the "openness of heart" named in the quote by Pope Francis (see pages 116–117) so that one can let go of assumptions, judgments, or anything that distracts from being fully present to the storyteller.

FOR DISCUSSION: *How do you see accompaniment linked to the mission of evangelization? How would you describe your abilities as an active listener?*

Regarding the segment "Step 5: The Art of Sacred Inquiry" *(pages 118–135)*

The process of accompaniment deepens through the process of sacred inquiry. After telling one's story, the seeker is encouraged to make deeper connections with their own faith and with the teachings of the Church, as well as scrutinizing the signs of the times and the culture. Huebsch emphasizes that the role of the accompanist at this point is "to walk with but not dominate the seeker in his or her discernment" (page 133).

FOR DISCUSSION: *How confident do you feel in your ability to lead another person into sacred inquiry? At what point might you need to refer the seeker to someone who is certified as a spiritual director or to seek professional help when uncovering deep personal issues?*

Regarding the segment "Step 6: The Moment of Theological Reflection: Contemplation" *(page 135)*

As the seeker's spiritual life deepens, so, too, does the draw toward holiness. This takes seekers deeper into their own hearts where, along with the accompanist, they "assume a contemplative stance and learn to place themselves in a receptive posture that leads to discernment" (page 135).

FOR DISCUSSION: *Reflect on the way in which your own prayer life has deepened as a result of your sacred journey. How has your pastoral leadership afforded you opportunities to draw others into a richer experience of prayer?*

Regarding the segment "Step 7: Discernment and Decision" *(pages 136–142)*

Drawing upon the image of the prophet Elijah hearing the voice of God in the "sheer silence," Huebsch emphasizes, for both the seeker and the accompanist, the importance of listening through self-examination and introspection. This leads into the process of discernment, which might result in deeper clarity around one's decisions or in recognizing the need for seeking formal spiritual direction.

FOR DISCUSSION: *Read over the descriptions of desolation and consolation on pages 140–141. In what ways might you provide guidance for someone experiencing either one?*

Regarding the segment "Step 8: Healing and Restoration" (pages 142–143)

Healing might be a profound outcome of theological reflection that is done both intentionally and prayerfully. As Huebsch notes, this isn't therapy or psychoanalysis, both of which require trained professionals. "The primary goal is a faith response" (page 142).

FOR DISCUSSION: *Recall an experience in which you found healing. Was there someone who accompanied you along the way?*

Regarding the illustration "Wally and Helen," and chapter review (pages 143–148)

The account of a couple devastated by the suicide of their nephew provides a touching and helpful way to apply the process of accompaniment to a pastoral situation. This is followed by a summation of the steps that flowed from careful listening to another's story and then drawing the person toward discernment and integration with both the teachings of the Church and attentiveness to one's own conscience.

FOR DISCUSSION: *How would you assess the way in which Janice accompanied Wally and Helen in the illustration? What steps did she take that reflect your own approach to pastoral leadership?*

In summing up the chapter, Huebsch notes that accompanists "do not act alone, but in league with others" (page 148). What forms of evaluation and teamwork do you use as a pastoral team? How might you increase a sense of accountability as you develop your approach to accompaniment?

FINAL REFLECTION AND DISCUSSION: *Reflect on an experience in which you have accompanied another person in your role as a pastoral leader. After reading this chapter, how would you assess your act of accompaniment? Is there something you would do differently? In what way do you feel affirmed by the material in this chapter?*

SESSION 6

PART 6 – Becoming a Parish of Promise and Hope *(page 149)*

In preparation for this session, all participants are asked to read pages 149–191 before the session.

This chapter moves into a practical application of accompaniment as it relates to various ministries. Beginning with the parish as the locus for this effort, it explains how to incorporate various forms of accompaniment into ministries of liturgy, catechesis, sacramental preparation, and pastoral care.

> **FOR REFLECTION AND DISCUSSION:** *How is your parish already practicing some form of accompaniment through its programs and ministries? What more could it be doing?*

Regarding the segment "Section 1: The Parish is the Context" *(pages 150–151)*
Since the parish is the primary place in which most pastoral ministry is practiced, the art of accompaniment will necessarily involve all of its members in one way or another. Huebsch is careful to point out that this isn't a program but a shift in the way people regard their ministries: "We want to act as Jesus did. In fact, we want to act like Jesus, in place of Jesus, and with the hands and voice of Jesus" (page 151).

FOR DISCUSSION: *What would it mean to shift your pastoral leadership toward* *one of accompaniment? How ready is your parish for this model of pastoral leadership?*

Regarding the segment "Section 2: Forms of Accompaniment" (pages 152–158)

This section describes four common forms of accompaniment in a parish: the primary household relationship, faith formation, pastoral care, and parish-wide. The first three have more focused aspects that generally involve specific pastoral leaders. The fourth includes the parish at large and entails a general ambiance of welcome, inclusion, and hospitality.

FOR DISCUSSION: *Of the four forms of accompaniment, which one(s) involve your area of pastoral leadership? How applicable are the suggestions for accompaniment within your particular ministry? What would you add or change about them?*

Regarding the segment "Section 3: Moving Your Parish toward Accompaniment" (pages 158–165)

All too often a parish rates its "success" on numbers, such as Mass attendance, faith formation enrollment, or collection plate offerings. Quoting Pope Francis, Huebsch notes that these are "worldly" ways of measuring effectiveness toward the mission of the Church. "Serving the poor and wounded, providing people who will welcome people in Jesus' name . . . , serving the poor and broken in the neighborhood, and radiating joy and mercy: these are big goals for any parish" (page 159).

FOR DISCUSSION: *The move toward a parish of accompaniment involves learning, deciding, and planning together. How feasible is it for your parish to move in this direction? How might you take the first step?*

Regarding the segment "Section 4: Planning to Be a Parish of Accompaniment" (pages 165–191)

The idea of moving the entire parish into a model of accompaniment can be daunting, but Huebsch breaks it into six manageable areas: liturgy, reconciliation, religious education, pastoral care, marriage preparation, and opportunities for conversion. Within each of these are sub-sections that can then be approached in whatever way best fits the profile of a particular parish. An illustration around sacramental preparation shows how the process can work through the use of skilled accompanists and the use of face-to-face parent chats.

FOR DISCUSSION: *Read over the "Litany of Welcome" on pages 167–168. How would you adapt this welcome for the people and circumstances in your parish? In which of the six areas does your pastoral leadership fall? How might you practice accompaniment by using the suggestions provided in this chapter?*

In your parish, how feasible is it to follow the approach taken in the illustration of St. Mary's and the parent chats organized around preparation for First Communion or other sacraments? How might you use or adapt this approach in order to make the process more personable, welcoming, and inclusive of those coming to the parish for the celebration of the sacraments?

FINAL REFLECTION AND DISCUSSION: *As your reflection and study of* ***Promise and Hope*** *comes to a close, what are your biggest takeaways for yourself, for your pastoral team, and for your parish at large? (You might want to take a moment to go over the appendix on pages 192–196 to help with this reflection.)*

Conclusion and Next Steps

If reading the book together with other pastoral leaders from your parish, go around the circle and name the takeaways. Then discuss three or more steps you will take together to move toward becoming a parish of accompaniment,

If reading the book on your own, write down a five-step plan for developing your skills as an accompanist and how you will apply them to your area of pastoral leadership. Consider who you might approach for collaboration and support in this effort.